Original title:
Through the Fire

Copyright © 2024 Swan Charm
All rights reserved.

Author: Liina Liblikas
ISBN HARDBACK: 978-9916-79-188-2
ISBN PAPERBACK: 978-9916-79-189-9
ISBN EBOOK: 978-9916-79-190-5

Angels in the Scorching Light

In the glow of golden rays,
Heavenly hosts do sing and praise.
Their wings unfurl, a holy dance,
Guiding souls with every glance.

Through trials fierce, they stand so near,
In the fire, they calm our fear.
Voices whisper, soft yet bright,
Angels dwell in the scorching light.

Embers of the Eternal

In the hearth of faith, sparks arise,
Embers glow 'neath vast, dark skies.
Each flicker tells of ancient lore,
The warmth of love forevermore.

From ashes, new life starts to grow,
In the night, the spirit's glow.
Through trials faced, and burdens borne,
Embers of the eternal, reborn.

The Glimpse Beyond the Heat

In the flames, a vision clear,
A glimpse beyond our earthly fear.
What seems to burn, transforms to light,
In shadows deep, faith takes flight.

Through the smoke, the truth shines bright,
Grace and mercy hover in sight.
Darkness yields to heaven's might,
A promise found beyond the height.

Finding Peace in the Blaze

When fires rage and hearts are torn,
Seek the peace in every dawn.
Within the blaze, love finds a way,
To guide us through the darkest day.

Embrace the heat, let spirits soar,
In the struggle, we find the door.
With every trial, we grow wise,
Finding peace where passion lies.

In the Heart of the Blaze

In the heart of the blaze, we stand tall,
Faith ignites, answering the call.
With each flicker, our spirits rise,
In shadows cast, the truth lies.

Through trials fierce, in fire's glow,
Divine whispers in embers flow.
Our hearts ablaze, pure and bright,
Walk with me into the light.

In the heat of despair, we find grace,
Love undying, our sacred space.
Through burning pain, we are refined,
In the heart of the blaze, peace we find.

A Hearth of Healing

Gather near, by the hearth we sit,
In warmth of grace, our fears we quit.
Hands held tight, in silent prayer,
A haven built with love and care.

In shadows deep, the light breaks through,
Gentle whispers remind us true.
Broken souls find solace here,
In the hearth of healing, we draw near.

With every tear, our burdens shed,
In this refuge, hope is fed.
Together strong, hearts intertwined,
At the hearth of healing, peace we find.

The Flame of Transcendence

See the flame that rises high,
A beacon bright against the sky.
In its glow, we shed our chains,
From earthly bounds, our spirit gains.

With eyes uplifted, we embrace the fire,
In the heart's blaze, we lift higher.
Each flicker a step, each spark a chance,
In the dance of light, our souls prance.

Transcendence calls through trials and fears,
In the flame's warmth, we shed our tears.
United as one, in love's expanse,
We are reborn, in the flame's dance.

Charred Yet Cherished

From ashes rise, we find our place,
Charred and battered, yet full of grace.
In scars we wear, a story told,
Of battles fought, and hearts of gold.

Each crack a testament to the fight,
In brokenness, we find the light.
Cherished moments, though charred, remain,
In the heart of the storm, joy and pain.

Through fire's touch, we gain new sight,
Rebirth through struggle, taking flight.
Cherished souls, forever entwined,
In the charred beauty, love we find.

Ascending from the Flames

From ashes rise, a soul renewed,
In fiery trials, faith imbued.
The light ignites, the spirit soars,
In scorching love, the heart restores.

Through smoke and heat, the path divine,
Embers whisper, a sacred sign.
In fervent prayer, we seek the light,
Ascending high, through darkest night.

Voices lift, a melody bright,
As flames entwine, in glorious fight.
The forge of God, where hearts are tried,
In purity, we shall abide.

The Altar's Silent Blaze

Upon the stones, we gather here,
In hushed reverence, hearts sincere.
A flicker speaks of timeless grace,
The altar glows, a warm embrace.

Soft whispers rise, a fragrant prayer,
Each flame a hope, unspoken care.
In quietude, the spirit dwells,
In every spark, a tale it tells.

To worship here, beneath the glow,
Where holy embers gently flow.
In silence strong, our faith aligns,
The altar's blaze, a path that shines.

Dances of Divine Embers

In sacred rhythm, the flames do sway,
A dance of light, in night and day.
With every flicker, joy takes flight,
In divine embrace, we find our light.

Around the fire, with hearts aglow,
The spirit moves, a gentle flow.
Each glowing ember, a grace bestowed,
In dance of faith, love is bestowed.

We lift our hands, in harmony's sound,
In divine dance, we are unbound.
With ardent joy, we sing and pray,
Embers of peace, forever stay.

Vessels of Holiness and Heat

We are the vessels, formed by flame,
In sacred heat, we know His name.
Through trials faced, our spirits grow,
In vessels pure, His light will glow.

Each moment blessed, a chance to hear,
The burning call, we hold so dear.
In unity, we stand as one,
With hearts ablaze, till day is done.

Let rivers flow, of mercy's grace,
In every heart, find holy space.
Vessels of love, in heat we meet,
Together strong, our faith complete.

Chronicles of the Burned

In shadows deep, the flames do rise,
A tale of souls beneath dark skies.
Each heart a canvas, charred and clear,
Bearing the marks of love and fear.

From embers soft, a whisper calls,
In echoed pain, the spirit sprawls.
Through trial's grip, the truth ignites,
A boundless spark that dare not fright.

With every scar, a lesson grows,
In hallowed hearts, the river flows.
Revived by grace, the ashes dance,
In every loss, a second chance.

Radiance in the Depths of Trial

When valleys low engulf the light,
And storms embrace the heart with fright,
There shines a glow, a beacon bright,
Drawing the weary toward the height.

Amidst the trials, faith sustains,
In darkest hours, love remains.
Each tear that falls, a seed of hope,
In sorrow's grip, our spirits cope.

The road is rough, the night is long,
Yet in these hymns, we find our song.
With every step, we rise anew,
In struggles faced, our strength is true.

Flames of Faith and Forgiveness

From ashes birthed, the fire blazes,
In hearts once lost, grace gently raises.
Through flames of faith, we learn to yield,
In seeds of mercy, love is healed.

Forgiving hands reach out in trust,
Turning to hope from bitter dust.
Through fiery trials, we emerge,
In humble hearts, deep love can surge.

With every crack, a light shines forth,
In faith we find our truest worth.
Flames forge stronger bonds to last,
Through trials faced, we stand steadfast.

Light from the Smoldering Ash

In smoldering ash, the spirit wakes,
From darkness deep, the heart remakes.
A flicker bright in night's embrace,
Illumes the path with gentle grace.

Out of the wreckage, hope arises,
In whispered truths, our soul surprises.
Each breath a prayer, each step a way,
To find the dawn of a brand new day.

So let the light break through the night,
In every soul, a spark of might.
For in the dark, we learn to see,
The smoldering ash shall set us free.

In the Light of the Crucible

In the silence of the night,
Faith is a guiding star.
Through trials we hold tight,
Each wound a sacred scar.

In the light of the flame,
Purity will arise.
Testing the heart's true name,
Where truth never lies.

Beneath the weight of sin,
The spirit finds its grace.
In suffering we begin,
To seek a holy place.

When doubt clouds the mind,
Hope shines brighter still.
In love we are entwined,
A testament of will.

In the embrace of loss,
We learn to let go.
Carrying our own cross,
In faith we come to know.

Fiery Lessons of the Spirit

Through the furnace we tread,
Lessons carved in flame.
In trials we are led,
To call His holy name.

The heart, tempered and bold,
Burns with love's pure heat.
In stories yet untold,
Our flesh and spirit meet.

Each sorrow, a guide's hand,
Leading us to the light.
In darkness, we shall stand,
With faith, our hearts ignite.

Beneath the sacred fire,
Resilience takes its hold.
In anguish we aspire,
To rise like saints of old.

With devotion, we take flight,
Spirits ready to soar.
In the radiant night,
We are forever more.

Sanctified by Sacred Heat

In the warmth of His love,
Cleansed by the holy flame.
From below and above,
We call upon His name.

Each trial, a holy rite,
Forging the spirit's core.
To cast shadows to light,
And open heaven's door.

In the crucible's embrace,
Fears dissolve and fall.
In our hearts, there's space,
To answer the divine call.

With every holy breath,
We ponder endless grace.
Beyond the veil of death,
In faith, we find our place.

Sanctuary in strife,
Our souls forever free.
Through pain, we find life,
In sacred unity.

The Purity of the Searing

In every searing test,
The soul finds its own way.
In burning, we are blessed,
Transformed by light of day.

Through trials, wisdom grows,
In ashes, hope is found.
Each ending also shows,
The scars that grace abound.

From fire, we are made whole,
Resilient and refined.
In strife, we trace our role,
With purpose intertwined.

In the depths of despair,
The spirit learns to sing.
Each burden, a shared care,
A dance with the divine king.

Through the flames, we do soar,
Our hearts forever bright.
In love, we endure more,
Guided by holy light.

From Ashes to Everlasting

From ashes we rise, hearts aflame,
In shadows we seek the holy name.
With courage we walk through trials of night,
Embracing the dawn, finding our light.

Through valleys of sorrow, we journey on,
Each step a promise, each tear a song.
In grace we stand, the burden is light,
Transformed by love, we soar into flight.

In hands of the faithful, hope is made whole,
Through suffering's forge, emerges the soul.
With faith as our anchor, we'll never part,
From ashes we rise, united in heart.

The Baptism by Radiance

In waters so deep, purity flows,
The Spirit descends, as ancient wind blows.
With reverence we bow, our hearts intertwined,
Baptized by radiance, our souls aligned.

The light breaks the silence, a whisper of grace,
With each drop of water, we find our place.
Emerging anew, we're cleansed and we're free,
In love's gentle currents, we find the key.

Through trials we wander, but never alone,
The light of His promise, in our hearts grown.
Our burdens are lifted, our spirits arise,
In faith we are woven, beneath endless skies.

Luminous Trials of the Soul

Through luminous trials, our spirits are tried,
In shadows we wander, but never denied.
Each challenge a blessing, in faith we must stand,
With hope as our lantern, we walk hand in hand.

The fire of trials burns bright in the night,
Yet love's gentle whisper guides us to light.
Each struggle a lesson, each tear a prayer,
In trials we flourish, through love we repair.

Embracing the journey, the path may be long,
In luminous trials, we uncover our song.
With every step closer to grace, we behold,
The radiant promise, in hearts brave and bold.

Of Flames and Faith

In flames of trial, our spirits ignite,
With faith as our shield, we embrace the light.
Through shadows of doubt, our courage will rise,
In the midst of the embers, our hearts find the skies.

With every flame kindled, a lesson unfolds,
Through pain we are tested, our strength becomes bold.
In the crucible fiery, our souls find their worth,
The ashes of struggle give way to new birth.

Of flames and of faith, we weave our own song,
For in every trial, we truly belong.
With love as our compass, we blaze a new trail,
In the journey of life, our spirits prevail.

When the Ember Calls

When the ember calls in the night,
With whispers soft, guiding light.
Hearts awaken to divine grace,
As souls gather in sacred space.

From shadows deep, we rise anew,
With faith restored, our spirits true.
In the warmth of love's embrace,
We journey forth, a holy race.

In the stillness, His voice we hear,
Echos of hope, casting out fear.
With every step, we tread the flame,
Igniting hearts in His holy name.

Bound by threads of celestial fire,
We seek the path that lifts us higher.
Through trials faced and sins confess'd,
In unity, our hearts find rest.

Oh, when the ember calls so sweet,
In every heart, the Savior meet.
Together we rise, under stars,
A chorus bright, erasing scars.

Refined in Heavenly Heat

In the furnace where love's embers glow,
We are shaped by trials, this we know.
Each flame a testimony bright,
In the dark, we find our light.

Refined like gold, through struggle we stand,
In the heat of trials, held by His hand.
With every breath, our spirits rise,
Transformed by faith, our hearts the prize.

Through storms we walk, unyielding faith,
In the crucible, we find our place.
Stronger now, with purpose clear,
Guided by love that casts out fear.

As the fire burns, our doubts release,
In surrender, we find sweet peace.
In heavenly heat, our souls unite,
To shine as stars in the endless night.

When the tempest rages and voices call,
We trust in the Lord, our all in all.
Refined in love, we boldly go,
Embracing grace wherever we flow.

Beneath the Sacred Ashes

Beneath the sacred ashes, lies,
The seeds of hope, where spirit flies.
In silence deep, the heart shall find,
Renewal born, a love unconfined.

Desire quenched by ashes' rest,
In quietude we find our best.
With faith as anchor, we arise,
To greet the dawn beneath bright skies.

In longing's pain, we see the way,
As light breaks forth to greet the day.
The ashes whisper of grace sublime,
In every heart, He writes His rhyme.

Here in the warmth of selfless care,
We gather strength through fervent prayer.
Together we rise, hand in hand,
Beneath the sacred, our spirits stand.

Oh, from the ashes, hope shall soar,
With love's embrace, forevermore.
Beneath the sacred ashes, we dwell,
United in hearts, our stories tell.

The Blazing Path of Redemption

On the blazing path, where sinners tread,
With heavy hearts and spirits fed.
In every step, forgiveness calls,
As mercy's light upon us falls.

Through shadows deep, His love will guide,
With every tear, our hearts abide.
On this journey, grace we seek,
In humility, we find the meek.

The blazing path, a road of truth,
In every trial, we reclaim youth.
With each burden lifted in strife,
In the arms of grace, we find our life.

As flames dance bright, our spirits soar,
In redemptive love, we're made once more.
The lighter load, as burdens cease,
In faith's embrace, we find our peace.

Oh, on this path, our souls ignite,
With love as guide, we break the night.
On the blazing road, forever strive,
In redemption's hope, our hearts alive.

Where the Fire Beckons

In the stillness of night's embrace,
I hear a call, a sacred place.
The flames arise, a guiding light,
Leading my heart through darkest flight.

The warmth, it whispers of divine grace,
A flickering love, time cannot erase.
With every spark, my spirit sings,
Of hope and peace, this fire brings.

Gathered round the holy blaze,
Lost souls find comfort, sing their praise.
In the dance of shadows, spirits soar,
Where the fire beckons, forevermore.

Holy Ember's Transformation

From ashes rise the holy spark,
Transforming shadows, illuminating dark.
In the glow of love's warm skin,
The holy ember draws us in.

Each flicker tells a story past,
Of hearts renewed, of chains uncast.
In every flame, a prayer aflight,
Wings of faith, taking to the night.

Life's sacred dance, we join as one,
Under the gaze of the radiant sun.
In the warmth, our souls entwine,
Holy ember, forever divine.

The Fiery Embrace of Mercy

In the garden of grace, fire softly glows,
Embracing the weary, where compassion flows.
The flames of mercy, a gentle tide,
In this fiery embrace, our fears subside.

With every flicker reflects the heart,
In radiant love, we play our part.
A sanctuary found in the heat,
As mercy and kindness, together meet.

In the warmth, we find our peace,
The fiery embrace will never cease.
Together we rise, renewed and blessed,
In love's great mercy, forever confessed.

Celestial Sparks in Darkness

Amidst the night, the stars ignite,
Celestial sparks pierce the fright.
Each twinkle whispers a sacred song,
Guiding the lost and weary along.

In shadows deep, hope starts to bloom,
With every glimmer, dispelling gloom.
The heavens' light begins to play,
Leading our souls, come what may.

With every spark, a path is shown,
In darkest hours, we're never alone.
Celestial guides, in faith we trust,
Illuminate our hearts, pure and just.

Pilgrimage through Glowing Trials

Through valleys low, my feet do tread,
With faith as light, where shadows spread.
Each step a prayer, each breath a song,
In trials fierce, I will be strong.

The road is long, but I am blessed,
With guidance fierce, through every test.
In darkest nights, the stars will shine,
Each trial faced, I draw the line.

Mountains high and rivers wide,
With hope my shield, I will abide.
The flame of truth ignites my heart,
In every struggle, I won't part.

Though flames may rise and storms may brew,
With every step, my spirit grew.
In pilgrimage, I seek the grace,
Of love divine in every place.

An Offering to the Flame

At twilight's dawn, I light the fire,
An offering made to Heaven's choir.
With whispers soft, I raise my prayer,
To flames that dance with love and care.

In ember's glow, my hopes take flight,
A sacred bond in the still of night.
Each flicker bright, a story spoken,
In glowing heat, the chains are broken.

Cleansed by flames, I shed my fears,
Through trials faced, I've shed my tears.
In every breath, the spirit flows,
An offering pure, the heart bestows.

To flames that guide, I bow my head,
For in their warmth, I'm gently led.
In sacred glow, I find my way,
An offering made, with love I pray.

Between the Embers of Hope

Between the embers, dreams ignite,
In fragile hearts, the sparks take flight.
With whispers soft, the night unfolds,
A tapestry of tales retold.

In quiet stillness, hope finds ground,
Where weary hearts, in faith, are found.
Each flicker bright, a guiding light,
Through darkest hours, I chase the night.

In sacred bonds, we gather near,
Through trials faced, we conquer fear.
The flame of love, it warms the soul,
Between the embers, we are whole.

With every breath, we rise anew,
In unity, our strength imbues.
Through ashes past, our spirits soar,
Between the embers, we are more.

The Inferno of Righteousness

In righteous flames, the heart ignites,
With passion fierce, we seek the heights.
For every trial, a lesson learned,
In inferno's grasp, our spirits burned.

Through trials wrought, we find our way,
In darkness cloaked, we greet the day.
With every step, we claim our fight,
In fervent faith, we spread the light.

The inferno speaks of sacrifice,
A path of love, it does entice.
To rise above, we shed our pain,
In flames of valiance, hope will reign.

With courage bold, we chase the fire,
In righteous cause, we climb higher.
Through all the strife, our hearts will glow,
In inferno's dance, our spirits flow.

From Cinders Arises Hope

In shadows deep, the embers glow,
A whisper soft, the winds do blow.
From ashes gray, new life will spring,
In the heart of night, the dawn will sing.

Through trials vast, our spirits soar,
Each pain endured opens a door.
With faith as light, we rise above,
In every loss, we find our love.

The past may haunt, but cannot bind,
From broken dreams, new paths we find.
With every step, we build anew,
In cinders false, a world shines true.

The fire burns, but cannot last,
What once was gone, is now our past.
Hope's gentle flame ignites the night,
A beacon bold, a source of light.

So let us stand, both strong and brave,
For from the depths, our souls we save.
In every heart, a spark remains,
From cinders old, new hope sustains.

The Radiance of Trial

In every test, a truth will gleam,
A silver thread, the Spirit's dream.
Through storms of doubt, our hearts will sway,
Yet in the struggle, light finds way.

The mountains high, the valleys low,
In every trial, our faith will grow.
With heavy burdens, we learn to fly,
Transcending pain, we touch the sky.

Each shadow casts a lesson bold,
In tales of pain, our hearts unfold.
From fiery trials, the soul takes flight,
Emerging pure, transformed by light.

In faith we walk, though paths may bend,
Each twist and turn, a means to mend.
The radiance within shines bright,
Guiding our way from night to light.

So let us cherish what we face,
For trials shape our sacred space.
With every dawn, a new chance starts,
In love and faith, we join our hearts.

Becoming Flame-Kissed

In fire's embrace, we learn to dance,
With every spark, we take a chance.
From fleeting flames, our spirits rise,
Becoming whole beneath the skies.

The warmth it brings, a sacred grace,
In every flicker, we find our place.
Through trials fierce, our souls align,
Becoming flame-kissed, we brightly shine.

Each ember's glow, a guiding star,
In darkest nights, it's never far.
With fierce resolve, we forge our way,
In every heartbeat, hope will stay.

As ashes fall, the past we shed,
What once was lost is now our thread.
In flames reborn, we rise anew,
With courage deep, we seek the true.

So let us burn with wisdom's light,
In every moment, wrong or right.
For in the fire, we find our fate,
Becoming flame-kissed, we celebrate.

Songs of the Scorched

In fields of sorrow, we lift our voice,
For in the pain, we find our choice.
The songs we sing are born of strife,
In rhythms raw, we share our life.

The ashes fall like gentle rain,
Each tear a testament of pain.
Yet from the burn, a chorus flows,
In every heart, a resilience grows.

With fervent hearts, we rise and share,
The songs of hope, we boldly bear.
In unity, we stand as one,
The scorched reclaim what's come undone.

From wounds we've healed, our voices soar,
In melodies sweet, we seek for more.
The past may haunt, but hope is strong,
Together we shall sing our song.

So let us cherish what we've learned,
In every heart, the flame is turned.
For songs of the scorched will ever be,
A testament to our victory.

Silhouettes in Holy Fire

In the quiet night, shadows dance,
Illuminated by a sacred glance.
Whispers of angels call us near,
In the warmth of faith, we persevere.

Glimmers of hope in the dark will show,
Lost souls find peace in the sacred glow.
Hands raised in prayer, hearts open wide,
In silhouettes, our spirits abide.

Fires of love ignite the dawn,
Beneath the stars, our troubles are gone.
Each flicker a promise, every spark a sign,
In the holy blaze, our lives entwine.

As we gather close in reverent grace,
To seek the truth and embrace solace.
In holy fire, our burdens light,
We walk hand in hand through endless night.

Let the flames guide us, a beacon so bright,
In unity, we find our sacred right.
Silhouettes merging, souls set free,
In the heart of the fire, we are meant to be.

Radiant Shadows of the Heart

In the garden where faith blooms bright,
Shadows dance with divine delight.
Each petal shines with a holy spark,
Radiant whispers light up the dark.

A gentle breeze carries prayers above,
In each heartbeat, a story of love.
As shadows weave through life's entwined path,
We find our strength in celestial wrath.

Through trials faced, darkness felt,

dimmed not the light, nor wrath that deals.
Radiant hope in every tear shed,
In shadows' embrace, we are gently led.

With every sorrow, a dawn does arise,
In the depths of despair, we shall rise.
Like shadows fading, fears take flight,
Radiant are hearts drawn to the light.

In every silence, echoes of grace,
A tapestry woven, in time and space.
Radiant shadows, forever we'll sing,
In the heart of the storm, peace may spring.

The Sacrificial Light

In the garden of sacrifice, we kneel,
With open hearts, we learn to feel.
Each drop of mercy, each gentle sigh,
A luminous path that leads us high.

Beneath the burden, our spirits soar,
In the act of giving, we find our core.
The light of love shines through the pain,
In every loss, there's much to gain.

Carved in the silence, a story unfolds,
Of courage and grace, a light that holds.
Through trials faced, we come to know,
In sacrificial love, our souls will grow.

As we gather close in solemn prayer,
The warmth of forgiveness fills the air.
In the glow of kindness, hearts ignite,
Transforming darkness with sacrificial light.

With hands extended, let us impart,
A beacon of hope from each loving heart.
The sacrificial light shall always shine,
Guiding us home, through the divine.

Destiny Carved in Fire

In the flames of fate, our paths are drawn,
Words etched in embers, from dusk till dawn.
Each crackle a promise, every glow a sign,
In the heart of chaos, we find the divine.

With courage kindled, we embrace the blaze,
Fires of destiny, through the mazes we gaze.
In each flicker, a vision bestowed,
On the road less traveled, our spirits flowed.

Through trials of life, our spirits ascend,
With faith as our guide, we reach around bends.
Carved in the fire, our stories entwine,
In the rhythm of time, our lives align.

In mirth and sorrow, we rise and we fall,
A tapestry woven, one thread and call.
Destiny dances in the flames we share,
In the heart of the fire, we find the rare.

Each flame ignites, a legacy's spark,
In unity, we navigate the dark.
Destiny carved in fire and light,
Together we walk toward the endless night.

Burning Away the Veil

In the quiet grove, whispers call,
Flames of truth begin to rise,
Veils of shadow gently fall,
Revealing wonder in the skies.

Cleansing fire dances bright,
Purging doubts with holy grace,
Hearts converge in sacred light,
Finding strength in love's embrace.

As the embers softly glow,
Wisdom flows through tepid night,
Guiding souls who seek to know,
The path of faith, the way of light.

In the ashes, hope is found,
Buried treasures, bold and rare,
With each flicker, truth unbound,
The veil lifts, love's breath in air.

Burning brightly, spirits soar,
With each flame, a voice sings free,
Together, we shall seek and explore,
Eternal light's shared destiny.

The Sanctity of Searing Light

In the dawn, the light is born,
A blazing truth that pierces night,
With each ray, new hope is sworn,
Sanctity wrapped in purest light.

From the depth of skies above,
Heaven whispers, soft and near,
Guiding us with boundless love,
Illuminating every fear.

In the flame, we feel the grace,
Searing wounds begin to heal,
In this light, we find our place,
With each moment, hearts reveal.

Cleansed by fire, spirits rise,
Embers dance upon the ground,
Hail the sun, eternal prize,
In its warmth, our truth is found.

Sacred light, forever true,
Piercing dark with holy breath,
All are called to start anew,
In the flame that conquers death.

Light for the Desperate Heart

In the shadows, whispers creep,
Desperate hearts find solace near,
With His light, they softly weep,
Finding strength to cast out fear.

Candle burning in the night,
Flickering hope within the soul,
Guiding lost to pure delight,
Mending hearts that yearn for whole.

With each spark, despair recedes,
Faith ignites in darkest times,
Love, the light the spirit needs,
A melody of sacred rhymes.

In the stillness, prayers ascend,
Wings of grace, they rise and soar,
Through the night, this love will blend,
Bringing hearts to safety's shore.

For the desperate, light shall shine,
Brighter than the stars above,
In the dark, their fates entwined,
Realizing they're wrapped in love.

Forgiveness in the Embers

In the hearth, old grudges fade,
Embers whisper, soft and low,
Through the fire, peace is made,
Teaching hearts to let love grow.

Forgive the scars that bind us close,
In this flame, we find release,
Through the heat, our spirits dose,
Warming souls with tender peace.

As the flame begins to dance,
We exchange our heavy chains,
In the glow, we take the chance,
To embrace joy, lose the pains.

With each spark, a promise born,
To uplift, to heal, to mend,
In the night, His heart is worn,
Forgiveness shines, the truest friend.

So let the embers guide our way,
Through the trials, come what may,
Together we shall choose the light,
In forgiveness, we find our might.

The Celestial Heat

In silence, the stars ignite,
Whispering warmth through the night.
They dance with grace, divine and bold,
In their glow, a story unfolds.

Each spark a dream, a prayer sent high,
Guiding souls like birds in the sky.
With every ember, hope is sown,
In celestial light, we are never alone.

Embrace the heat, let it refine,
Transform your fears into the divine.
For in the flame, we find our way,
Turning shadows into bright day.

Through trials faced, we rise anew,
With hearts ignited and spirits true.
In the blaze of faith, we stand strong,
Together we sing our sacred song.

From Fire's Embrace to Faith's Strength

From embers we rise, forged in the fire,
Burning away all doubt and desire.
With every trial, our spirits ignite,
In this embrace, we find our true light.

The flame that consumes, also refines,
In its heat, our purpose aligns.
From ashes of loss, we gather our gains,
In the heart of the fire, hope remains.

Faith like a candle, flickers and glows,
Strengthened by storms, as the wind blows.
Through darkest nights, we hold on tight,
To the promise of dawn, shining bright.

Each spark of love, a beacon of grace,
In life's trials, we find our place.
Together we emerge, hand in hand,
From fire's embrace, we rise and stand.

Trials of the Flame

In the furnace of life, we learn to be bold,
Each trial a tale waiting to be told.
Adversity's grip may tighten its hold,
But in every struggle, our spirits unfold.

When the flames of doubt flicker high,
We look for the strength that will not die.
For in this heat, we shape our fate,
With courage ignited, we rise from hate.

Purified through the trials we meet,
Each scar a badge, each challenge a feat.
In the face of anguish, we find our way,
In the heart of the flame, we learn to pray.

So let the fire burn bright as the sun,
With love as our shield, and faith as our gun.
Together we conquer, together we stand,
In the trials of flame, we are blessed and unplanned.

In the Crucible of Grace

In the crucible's warmth, our souls intertwine,
Forged by the trials, in love we align.
Through the heat of the moment, we grow ever near,
In the silence of grace, we cast aside fear.

With each passing day, the pressure may mount,
Yet faith is our anchor, our sacred account.
In the furnace of life, together we strive,
In the crucible of grace, our dreams come alive.

From darkness to light, we carve our own way,
With hearts full of hope, we gather to pray.
In the embrace of the flame, we learn to be free,
In the crucible's fire, our spirits agree.

So stand by my side as we face what may come,
In grace, we are stronger, together as one.
Through trials and triumphs, we rise from despair,
In the crucible of grace, our burdens we share.

The Glimmers of Grace

In quiet whispers of the night,
The stars above begin to shine.
Each spark a promise, pure and bright,
A gentle touch of the divine.

Through valleys deep and shadows cast,
A flicker shows the path ahead.
With faith, we'll rise, our shadows passed,
In grace, our spirits are fed.

The dawn awakens with a song,
Each note a solace, soft and true.
In every moment, we belong,
For love shines down from skies of blue.

With open hearts, we stand as one,
Embracing light that breaks the night.
With every day, new grace begun,
We walk by faith, not by our sight.

In glimmers small, His love appears,
A guiding flame, a radiant guide.
Through every trial, through our fears,
We find in Him, our hearts abide.

Devotion Forged in Fire

In trials fierce, our faith does grow,
Like metal shaped upon the wheel.
Through flames we pass, our spirits glow,
In love's embrace, our wounds will heal.

The darkest nights bring forth the dawn,
A testament of strength and grace.
Each struggle faced, a battle won,
With steadfast hearts, we seek His face.

In unity, we rise anew,
Each tear a prayer, each sigh a song.
Together, we will see it through,
In perfect love, we all belong.

The forge of life, it tempers souls,
With every trial, we endure.
In sacrifice, devotion rolls,
A sacred bond that shall be pure.

Through fires bright, our spirits soar,
Transformed by grace, awakened strong.
In every heart, His love will pour,
Together, we will carry on.

The Radiant Journey

With every step upon this way,
A light unfolds before our eyes.
We walk in faith, come what may,
Our hearts uplifted to the skies.

Through rugged paths and gentle streams,
Each moment holds a gift of grace.
In every breath, we weave our dreams,
A sacred dance in His embrace.

When storms arise and shadows loom,
Our souls will find the strength to rise.
In darkness blooms a fragrant bloom,
His love, a light that never dies.

Together on this sacred quest,
We lift our voices to the sky.
In each challenge, we are blessed,
With courage found, our spirits fly.

The journey calls, a sacred song,
In unity, our hearts align.
With every step, we grow more strong,
Embracing love, our spirits shine.

Hearts Kindled in Trials

When shadows fall and doubts arise,
In trials deep, our faith stands tall.
With every tear, our spirit cries,
Yet love rejoices through it all.

For in the fire, our hearts refine,
Like gold that's tempered in the blaze.
In darkest hours, His light will shine,
Illuminating all our ways.

We gather close, our hands entwined,
Each story told, a thread of grace.
In every struggle, wisdom find,
Together, we embrace the space.

The storms may rage, the winds may howl,
Yet anchored firm, our souls will stand.
With faith as guide, we hear the howl,
In love's embrace, we clasp His hand.

Through every trial, hearts ignite,
Kindled by hope, we rise anew.
In unity, we share the light,
With fervent hearts, we find what's true.

The Seeker's Dance with Flames

In shadows deep, a heart does yearn,
To seek the truth, to seek the burn.
With every step, a spirit's flight,
In flames of hope, I chase the light.

Each flicker whispers secrets old,
Of stories told, of glories bold.
The fire sways, a sacred trance,
In sacred rhythm, my soul's dance.

The night may chill, the winds will bite,
Yet in my chest, a flickering light.
I bow to flames, my humble plea,
In their embrace, I long to be.

With every spark, a lesson learned,
In passion's blaze, my heart is burned.
What once was fear, now turns to grace,
In the pure heat, I find my place.

So let the flames endure my fate,
Within their warmth, I meditate.
The seeker's journey, bold and bright,
In fire's dance, I find my might.

Radiant Afflictions of the Soul

In anguish deep, the spirit cries,
Yet through the tears, the soul will rise.
Each pain a shade, a story spun,
In suffering's heart, the light's begun.

Afflictions press, like weights of stone,
Yet in their grasp, I feel not alone.
For in each struggle, grace unfolds,
A tapestry of faith, retold.

With every wound, a lesson sown,
In depth of night, the seeds are grown.
Radiant strength from shadows cast,
In trials faced, my spirit fast.

I rise to greet the dawning day,
With every sigh, I earn my way.
Illuminated by a steadfast hope,
Through burdens borne, my soul can cope.

In radiant hues, the spirit glows,
Transforming pain, where love now flows.
From darkest nights, to brightest morn,
Afflictions fade, new life is born.

The Flames of Divine Love

In every heart, a fire ignites,
A sacred spark, through days and nights.
This flame divine, it guides my way,
In love's embrace, I long to stay.

With whispers soft, and burning craze,
It warms my soul, in endless praise.
Through trials faced, it swells and grows,
A radiant force, that softly glows.

From highest peaks to valleys low,
In love's pure fire, I come to know.
The warmth it gives, the light it shares,
In every breath, my spirit dares.

Through storms of doubt, my heart will stand,
Embracing flames, my soul's command.
For in this heat, divine and bright,
I find my truth, my endless light.

Oh, flames of love, forever blaze,
Illuminate my path with grace.
In you, I trust, in you, I find,
The perfect peace of heart and mind.

Reflections in the Firelight

As embers dance, they truthfully show,
The stories held in fire's glow.
Reflections flicker, shapes and forms,
In every spark, my spirit warms.

What secrets lie in flames of old?
In whispered tales, the past unfolds.
Each firelight flicker, a voice divine,
Guiding my heart, through space and time.

Beneath the stars, in night's embrace,
I seek the depth, I crave the grace.
In fire's warmth, my fears subside,
With open heart, I turn inside.

These radiant beams, they softly tell,
Of heaven's kiss and earth's sweet swell.
In silence deep, reflections sway,
In fire's light, I find my way.

So let me sit, and watch the flames,
In their warm dance, I call your name.
With every flicker, peace I bind,
In firelight's glow, my soul aligned.

In the Wake of the Radiance

In the stillness of dawn's embrace,
Whispers of grace fill the space.
Heaven's breath calms the soul,
Guiding hearts toward their goal.

Each spark ignites a sacred flame,
Awakening love, calling His name.
In shadows cast by yesterday's sins,
A light arises, new life begins.

Wounds of the past, healed by the light,
Hope blooms anew, dispelling the night.
Faith is the anchor, steadfast and true,
In the wake of radiance, we are renewed.

Hands lifted high in humble praise,
Instruments of peace through our days.
Carried forth by a spirit divine,
Together we stand, forever aligned.

Silent prayers drift on the breeze,
A symphony flows through the trees.
In unity's bond, our hearts take flight,
In the wake of the radiance, all is made right.

Sanctified by the Inferno

Through raging flames, a path is forged,
In trials faced, our spirits enlarged.
Refined by fire, we rise and sing,
Sanctified by the lessons it brings.

From ashes we bloom, a testament true,
In fervent embrace, we are made anew.
God's love, a beacon, shining so bright,
Guiding our hearts from darkness to light.

Moments of doubt, we carry with grace,
Each tempest endured, a sacred space.
As embers dance in the cool of the night,
We gather strength in the warmth of the light.

In the heart of the storm, we find our peace,
The inferno's call leads to sweet release.
In this holy blaze, we willingly tread,
For through every trial, our fears are shed.

Embrace the fire, let it ignite,
A fervent love that conquers the night.
We walk hand in hand, in love's gentle flow,
Sanctified by the inferno we know.

The Purifying Heat

In the furnace of trials, we learn to endure,
The purifying heat makes the spirit pure.
Each drop of sweat, a tear of the soul,
Cleansing the heart, making us whole.

Through struggles faced, we find our might,
In shadows we walk, seeking the light.
With every breath, our resolve renews,
In the fires of faith, we are born and we choose.

Let our hearts blaze with a fervent fire,
With love as our guide, we shall never tire.
Companions in struggle, hand in hand clasped,
Through the purifying heat, our spirits are grasped.

As winds of change sweep over the land,
We lift our voices, united we stand.
In the trials we face, His promise we keep,
For in the purifying heat, our souls gently leap.

The warmth of His promise shines ever bright,
In the depths of despair, we hold to the light.
Through life's raging storm, we shall find our seat,
In the embrace of the purifying heat.

Divine Light Among the Cinders

In the remnants of what once was whole,
Divine light beckons, healing the soul.
Among the cinders, hope starts to gleam,
Illuminating paths where shadows redeem.

Each flicker glows with a story untold,
Whispers of love in the ashes unfold.
With every heartbeat, His grace we find,
A tapestry woven, in spirit aligned.

Through darkest nights, we learn to be brave,
For in our struggles, we're crafted, not enslaved.
Like stars in the sky, our spirits take flight,
Transformed by the fire, embracing the light.

The past may linger, but we shall rise,
With divine guidance, we open our eyes.
In the stillness, His presence we trace,
Among the cinders, we feel His embrace.

Journeying forth, ignited by grace,
In unity's warmth, we find our place.
With hearts illuminated, we strive and we dare,
Divine light among the cinders, forever we share.

The Crucible's Call

In trials deep, the soul must stand,
Through fire's test, we take His hand.
With faith as firm as ancient stone,
In darkest night, we're not alone.

The embers glow, a sacred sign,
In every heart, His light will shine.
The crucible, our path divine,
We rise in strength, His love our line.

Through pain and strife, we come to know,
The depth of love, the grace we show.
Each wound a mark, each scar a thread,
In woven hearts, His spirit led.

With weary eyes, we seek the dawn,
In shadows cast, our fears withdrawn.
A whispered prayer, a hopeful song,
In unity, we all belong.

So let us walk with heads held high,
With trust in Him, we will not shy.
Through every trial, our spirits free,
The crucible leads us to be He.

Elysian Fire

In realms above, where angels soar,
The fire ignites, forevermore.
A dance of light, a holy flame,
In hearts aflame, we praise His name.

Elysian fire, pure and bright,
Guides weary souls through darkest night.
With every spark, a prayer ascends,
In sacred trust, our spirit mends.

The warmth we feel, a gentle grace,
In every breath, we find our place.
Through trials faced, we rise anew,
In love's embrace, we learn what's true.

Let not despair consume the heart,
From ashes rise, we make a start.
With every moment, hope we find,
In Elysian fire, hearts entwined.

Together bound, we seek the peace,
With faith we walk, our fears release.
In unity, our spirits soar,
Elysian fire forevermore.

Renewed in Radiance

Awake, O heart, to morning's grace,
In every dawn, a light we trace.
Renewed in radiance, spirit bright,
With every step, we chase the light.

The burdens lift, the shadows flee,
In faith we stand, in love set free.
We seek the path that He has laid,
With every moment, hope displayed.

In quiet whispers, truth revealed,
Through trials faced, our wounds are healed.
The journey long, but heart aglow,
Renewed in grace, we come to know.

With open arms, we greet the day,
In every prayer, we find our way.
Each breath a gift, each moment rare,
In radiant love, we find our care.

So shine, O light, within us bright,
In every heart, ignite the night.
We walk this path, both strong and true,
Renewed in radiance, all made new.

Sacred Flames of Truth

In every heart, a flame does burn,
The sacred truth, we must discern.
With faith as anchor, hope our guide,
In holy light, we shall abide.

The flames of love, they rise and sing,
In every soul, a heavenly spring.
With open eyes, we seek the way,
In each embrace, His love shall stay.

In trials faced, the fire won't dim,
With courage bold, our spirits brim.
Through darkest nights, we stand as one,
Until the day of victory's sun.

The sacred flames, they dance and play,
A light for all who seek His way.
With each spoken word, a prayer anew,
In every heart, His truth breaks through.

So let us gather, hand in hand,
With sacred flames, our spirits stand.
Together bound, we rise in grace,
In sacred flames, we find our place.

Forged in Passionate Light

In the glow of dawn's embrace,
Hearts awaken with sacred grace.
Each breath a hymn, a soul set free,
Bound by love's unwavering decree.

Light spills forth on paths divine,
Guiding us with sacred signs.
Through trials fierce, we rise and stand,
In passionate light, held by His hand.

Where shadows linger, hope ignites,
Illuminating darkest nights.
With every prayer, we find our might,
Forged anew in this holy light.

In unity, we walk the way,
Together strong, come what may.
With faith as our eternal guide,
In passionate light, we shall abide.

Let spirits soar on winds of grace,
And in His love, we find our place.
For in this journey, hearts align,
Forged in the light, forever shine.

Seraphic Flames in Shadows

In shadows deep, where silence dwells,
A whisper stirs, as the spirit tells.
Seraphic flames begin to rise,
Illuminating truth from skies.

With every flicker, hope is found,
In the quiet, grace abound.
Through darkest nights, love leads the way,
Seraphic flames, come light the day.

Hearts entwined in sacred fire,
Burning bright with pure desire.
In trials faced, we shall embrace,
The warmth of love, the light of grace.

As shadows dance, we stand in trust,
In seraphic flames, we find our thrust.
For through the night, our spirits soar,
Ever in light, forevermore.

In the witness of the stars, we rise,
Awake, alive, 'neath endless skies.
With every flame that touches cold,
We shine with love, our hearts unfold.

Flame-touched Pathways of the Spirit

On pathways tread where spirits roam,
Each step a prayer, leading home.
Flame-touched hearts, in love's embrace,
Awakened souls, a sacred space.

As candles burn with gentle glow,
Wisdom's whispers softly flow.
Through winding roads, our spirits sing,
To hope and faith, we shall cling.

In every trial, a lesson learned,
Through flame's caress, our passion burned.
With every dawn, a chance to rise,
To walk in light, beneath vast skies.

The spirit's dance in twilight's hue,
A flame ignited, pure and true.
With every breath, we find our way,
On flame-touched paths, we choose to stay.

Together, hand in hand we move,
In love's pure light, we find our groove.
For in this journey, hearts aligned,
In flame's embrace, our souls combined.

The Candle's Quiet Courage

In the stillness, a candle glows,
Casting warmth where the spirit flows.
With quiet courage, it stands tall,
A beacon bright, to guide us all.

In flickers soft, a promise made,
Through darkest trials, unafraid.
Igniting hearts with gentle grace,
The candle's glow, a warm embrace.

As shadows creep and doubts assail,
Its light persists, a silent tale.
With every flicker, peace descends,
In quiet strength, the spirit mends.

Through storms that shake, we find our ground,
In each small flame, a power found.
The candle speaks of love and trust,
A quiet courage, strong and just.

So let us shine in unity,
With every heart, in harmony.
For in the dark, we find our way,
The candle's courage lights the day.

The Celestial Forge

In the heart of the heavens divine,
Angels gather, their tasks entwine.
With each stroke, they craft the light,
From the essence of day and night.

Stars sing songs of fate unbent,
In the forge where the heavens are rent.
Souls are shaped from cosmic fire,
In the glow of eternal desire.

With hammers of hope and anvils of grace,
They mold the dreams in a sacred space.
For every heart that's been torn asunder,
Restoration blooms amidst the thunder.

Forging bonds that never break,
In this celestial dance we awake.
With every creation, the cosmos sways,
Echoing life through infinite days.

So rise from the dust, let your spirit soar,
In the celestial forge, forever explore.
For the light that you seek is born from within,
In the heart of the heavens, where all begins.

Rising from Fiery Shadows

Through shadows deep, where sorrows dwell,
Hope ignites like a distant bell.
From ashes rise the souls reborn,
As dawn unveils the golden morn.

With every trial, a lesson learned,
In the furnace of life, the spirit burned.
Forged in courage, we stand tall,
Embracing the light that pierces all.

Fear not the night, it yields to grace,
Every tear in time finds its place.
In fiery depths, the heart transcends,
With love as the flame, all sorrow mends.

From the ruins, the vision grows,
In the gaps where the divine flows.
Together we rise, hand in hand,
Through fiery shadows, our spirits stand.

Embrace the warmth that fuels the sky,
With every heartbeat, we learn to fly.
The dawn is a promise, eternally bright,
As we rise from shadows into the light.

Illuminated Destiny

In the quest of souls seeking truth,
A path emerges from the wisdom of youth.
Each step forward, a light bestowed,
In the silence, where dreams are sowed.

Guided by stars in a velvet night,
Our hearts aglow with an inner light.
Every choice a brush on the canvas wide,
Painting destinies where hopes abide.

With faith as our compass, we journey forth,
To uncover the treasures of our true worth.
Through trials faced, and paths we roam,
In the embrace of destiny, we find our home.

The winds of change may howl and roar,
Yet we stand firm on this sacred shore.
In illuminated moments, our spirits soar,
Connected by love forevermore.

Through every struggle, we rise and shine,
For the tapestry woven is yours and mine.
With hearts aligned in a cosmic dance,
In illuminated destiny, we find our chance.

The Lighthouse Beneath the Ashes

In the wreckage of dreams long past,
Amidst the ashes, a light holds fast.
The lighthouse flickers, a beacon bright,
Guiding the weary back toward light.

Through storms that rage and shadows that loom,
The heart's whisper cuts through the gloom.
A sanctuary built on hope's decree,
In the lighthouse, our spirits are free.

Where trials have burned what we thought defined,
New paths arise, with purpose aligned.
For every ember speaks of new birth,
In the depths of despair, we find our worth.

Stand tall, O soul, let your spirit sing,
A survivor's anthem, a sacred offering.
In the lighthouse beneath the ashes' embrace,
We find the divine in our sacred space.

So carry the light through depths unknown,
In the heart of darkness, no longer alone.
The lighthouse shines brighter as we ascend,
Transforming the night into love without end.

Witness to the Divine Fire

In the stillness of the night,
Bright embers dance and glow,
Hearts awake with sacred fire,
Touched by grace, our spirits flow.

Voices rise in fervent prayer,
Seeking truth in ancient lore,
Guided by the flames that share,
Wisdom found on heaven's shore.

Each flicker speaks, a story told,
Of love profound and trials faced,
In the warmth, our fears unfold,
In this light, our souls embraced.

Beneath the stars, we gather round,
To honor all that burns within,
Together here, forever bound,
In fervor, we let praises spin.

With every spark, a bond ignites,
A witness to the light's embrace,
In this dance of holy sights,
We find our way to sacred space.

The Reckoning of the Flame

In shadows deep, the flame does rise,
Awakening souls from blissful sleep,
Its fervor cuts through veils and lies,
Revealing secrets buried deep.

A reckoning within each heart,
The fire purges all that's worn,
Old chains are broke, new paths to chart,
Through the blaze, we are reborn.

In the heat of trials, strength will bloom,
With every pulse, the spirit sways,
Transformed by light, dispelling gloom,
In the ash, we find new ways.

The flame, it guides us like a star,
Illuminating life's frail thread,
With every flicker, we go far,
As love's foundation, never dead.

So let the fire dance and spin,
A promise bright, forever true,
In unity, we now begin,
The reckoning, our hearts anew.

Whispers of the Searing Light

In the silence, whispers play,
From searing light, we hear the call,
Each ray a pathway, guiding our way,
To rise above, to never fall.

The warmth of truth fills every space,
As shadows wane, the light extends,
Embracing all in loving grace,
In unity, our spirit mends.

With courage drawn from holy flame,
We step into the unknown night,
For in this blaze, we find a name,
A bond that's forged in sacred light.

Together, we shall journey far,
Through valleys dark and mountains high,
For every soul, a guiding star,
In whispers soft, our hearts reply.

So let us gather, hand in hand,
In the presence of the divine,
With searing light, we make our stand,
In love's embrace, forever shine.

The Divine Inferno Within

Deep within, the inferno burns,
A holy spark, eternal flame,
In silence, wisdom gently churns,
Awakening the heart to claim.

With fervent hearts, we gather round,
To stoke the fire, feed the spark,
In unity, in love, we're found,
Illuminating every dark.

This divine inferno knows no bounds,
It weaves through every soul it meets,
In every pulse, the sacred sounds,
A symphony that love completes.

Through trials faced, we rise anew,
Embracing all that life bestows,
With open hearts, and vision true,
In the inferno, our spirit glows.

So let us fan this holy fire,
With every breath, a prayer we send,
To lift us higher, to never tire,
The divine inferno, our eternal friend.

Through the Radiant Trials

In shadows deep, we walk with grace,
Guided by light in every space.
Through trials fierce, our hearts will rise,
Embraced by faith, our spirits wise.

With every tear, a lesson learned,
In every flame, our passion burned.
Together, we shall brave the night,
In radiant love, we find our light.

Though storms may rage and whispers taunt,
We stand as one, our souls enshrined.
For in the pain, we find our song,
With steadfast hope, we all belong.

The journey long, yet spirits soar,
Through trials wide, our hearts explore.
In every test, the truth we find,
Transcending fear, our will aligned.

With every step, we claim our fate,
With faith ablaze, we conquer hate.
Through radiant trials, we are reborn,
In love's embrace, forever sworn.

The Glowing Path

Where shadows fall, the light reveals,
A glowing path, our heart it heals.
With every step, the journey calls,
In unity, our spirit sprawls.

Through fields of grace and valleys wide,
With every breath, the truth our guide.
We walk with purpose, hand in hand,
In faith we trust, together stand.

The stars above, a map divine,
Illuminates the road we find.
Each challenge faced, a chance to grow,
In every trial, love's strength will show.

With open hearts, we seek the way,
Guided by light, we shall not stray.
Through every tear, the lessons flow,
In every joy, our spirits glow.

So let us tread this glowing ground,
In every soul, true peace is found.
Through love and light, our spirits soar,
On this path, forevermore.

Unyielding Spirit

In midst of trials, we hold the flame,
An unyielding spirit, we proclaim.
With steadfast hearts, we face the storm,
In love's embrace, our souls transform.

Through every doubt, our courage grows,
In faith's embrace, the ultimate rose.
We rise again, with voices strong,
In unity, we all belong.

The weight of sorrow, heavy yet bright,
In darkest hours, we find our light.
For in the struggle, strength is born,
From broken hearts, new dreams adorn.

With every step, we march with pride,
An unyielding spirit, as our guide.
Through trials faced, we shine and stand,
With love's pure light, we take command.

So let us sing, our voices clear,
In every moment, love draws near.
With unyielding spirit, we shall rise,
In unity, we touch the skies.

Alight with Purpose

In every heart ignites a flame,
Alight with purpose, life's sacred game.
With passion bright and dreams that soar,
A call to love, forevermore.

Through every moment, grace unfolds,
In kindness shared, a story told.
With courage strong, we face the day,
In every challenge, hope's array.

Our spirits dance in joy's embrace,
Alight with purpose, we find our place.
Through trials faced, we rise anew,
In love's foundation, us two as one.

With open arms, we greet the dawn,
Through every loss, a path redrawn.
Together we stand, hearts intertwined,
In love's pure light, we are defined.

So let our voices echo wide,
In every heart, pure love abide.
Alight with purpose, bold and free,
In unity's grace, we'll always be.

A Pilgrim's Inferno

In shadows deep, where sorrows dwell,
A pilgrim walks, with tales to tell.
Each step a prayer, each breath a plea,
In the fire's gloom, his soul is free.

Through trials fierce, the heart must strive,
To find the light, to feel alive.
With faith as guide, through darkest night,
He seeks the dawn, the coming light.

The flames of doubt, they flicker high,
Yet in their dance, he learns to fly.
With courage held, he faces fate,
For in the struggle, there's no hate.

The ashes fall, a sign of grace,
In every scar, a holy trace.
From anguish borne, a spirit soars,
In love's embrace, he finds the doors.

Each spark ignites a sacred spark,
In the inferno, he leaves a mark.
A pilgrim's heart, forever bright,
In endless quest, to seek the light.

The Blessed Blaze

In every heart the flame does glow,
A blessed blaze, a holy flow.
With hands uplifted, voices raise,
To honor Him, we sing His praise.

The fire of love, it warms the soul,
In trials faced, it makes us whole.
From every tear, a ember flies,
In darkness deep, the spirit tries.

With every breath, we fan the flame,
In joy and sorrow, call His name.
For in the heat, we find our place,
In fiery love, we see His face.

Let not the cold extinguish hope,
In His embrace, we learn to cope.
The blaze within, a guiding star,
In life's great quest, we journey far.

Together bound, we face the night,
In unity, our hearts take flight.
Through every trial, we shall remain,
The blessed blaze, our sacred flame.

Illumined in the Heat

In sacred fires, our spirits dance,
Illumined bright, we take our chance.
Through trials fierce, we learn to see,
The truth in flames, the path to be.

In every struggle, a lesson found,
With burning love, our hearts are bound.
From shadows cast, we rise anew,
Illumined souls, in light so true.

The warmth of faith, it lights the way,
In every night, it guides our day.
With hands held high, we speak His name,
In fellowship, we feed the flame.

For every scar, a mark of grace,
In trials faced, we find our place.
With every blaze, our souls combine,
Illumined hearts, in love we shine.

In unity, we share the light,
Through darkest paths, we forge our fight.
In sacred heat, we stand as one,
Illumined by the rising sun.

From Ashes to Ascendancy

From ashes bright, the phoenix sings,
In every heart, a new hope springs.
Through trials faced, the spirit soars,
From every end, new life restores.

In flames of pain, transformation's born,
With every wound, new wings adorn.
Through depths we dive, in light we trust,
From ashes rise, to fulfill our lust.

The path is fraught with fire and flame,
Yet from despair, we find our claim.
For every loss, a chance to grow,
From ashes deep, our courage glows.

In faith we walk, through darkest nights,
From barren grounds, we seek the heights.
With every step, ascend we must,
In love's embrace, we place our trust.

From shadows cast, to light we cling,
In unity, our voices ring.
With every heart, we rise anew,
From ashes to ascendancy, we pursue.

The Searing Path to Glory

In shadows cast by doubt and fear,
We walk the path that leads us near.
With eyes fixed on the distant light,
Our hearts ignite in faith's pure fight.

Through trials faced with steadfast grace,
We find the strength to run this race.
Each step a prayer, each breath a song,
For glory waits where we belong.

The road is steep, the burden great,
But love will guide, and hope will sate.
With every flame that tempts us bold,
We rise anew, our spirits hold.

In fervent faith, we seek the truth,
Embracing joy, forsaking ruth.
The searing trials polish bright,
Our souls transformed, our futures bright.

Through fires fierce, we learn to see,
The beauty held in destiny.
With hands uplifted, we rejoice,
In glory's name, we make our choice.

Allure of the Divine Heat

In morning mist, the warmth does rise,
A sacred call beneath the skies.
The flames of love my heart do greet,
In every pulse, the prayer's heartbeat.

The blaze that dances in the night,
A beacon bold, a guiding light.
With every flicker, every spark,
I find His presence in the dark.

With fervent zeal, my spirit spreads,
The allure of warmth that gently threads.
In whispers soft, my soul awakes,
In fiery grace, my journey takes.

From ashes rise, new life in sight,
The promise shining ever bright.
Through trials faced, my heart will sing,
In the divine, I find my king.

So let me walk in heat so pure,
With faith as my only cure.
Through every trial, every fate,
I yield to love, accept His state.

Flames of the Faithful Journey

Through valleys low and mountains tall,
We carry forth, responding to the call.
In flames that burn, but do not tire,
We find the strength to climb higher.

Each step we take, a sacred vow,
In trials faced, I kneel and bow.
The faithful journey carved in pain,
But through the fire, love's truth we gain.

The flames of hope, they dance and sway,
In darkest nights, they light the way.
Through every fear and every doubt,
A courage found, a voice to shout.

With fiery hearts, we praise His name,
In every challenge, we stake our claim.
For in this journey, we are one,
The flames unite us, 'til we're done.

So let the fire within us blaze,
As we walk forth in love's sweet haze.
With every spark, our spirits rise,
In faith's embrace, we touch the skies.

The Spirit's Fiery Ascent

From earthly binds, our spirits fly,
Like eagles soaring, up to the sky.
To realms where love and wisdom meet,
Our souls ignite, the journey sweet.

In rapture high, we find our place,
A sacred dance, God's warm embrace.
Through trials faced, we rise again,
To taste the joy of peace within.

The spirit's fire burns fierce and bright,
Illuminating every night.
With grateful hearts, we sing His praise,
In every trial, our faith we raise.

Through the ascent, our burdens cease,
In unity, we find our peace.
With every flame, transformation near,
The spirit's cry is crystal clear.

As we ascend the heights of grace,
In love's embrace, we find our space.
The journey long, but worth the cost,
In fiery ascent, we find the lost.

The Holy Trial

In the silence, shadows loom,
Faith is tested, hearts in bloom.
With every step, we seek the light,
Guided gently through the night.

Whispers echo, prayers arise,
In the storm, the spirit flies.
Through the struggle, truth will shine,
Love abounds, the path divine.

Beneath burdens, spirits soar,
Strengthen us, forevermore.
In the trial, find our grace,
Holy promise we embrace.

Hands uplifted, souls converge,
From each pain, new hope will surge.
In the fire, we are forged,
Life anew, we are restored.

Through each moment, faith does grow,
In the valley, rivers flow.
Together, we shall stand as one,
In the light of love begun.

Flames of Forgiveness

In the heart, a fire glows,
Burning bright, where mercy flows.
Let go of darkness, embrace the dawn,
In forgiveness, we are reborn.

Wounds may ache, but love will mend,
In His grace, we find our end.
Forgive them, Lord, for they know not,
In Your warmth, we are caught.

With each breath, release the pain,
Through the ashes, hope will reign.
Let grudges fall, the spirit rise,
In the light, compassion lies.

Boundless love breaks every chain,
From our hearts, all strife must wane.
In the fire, hearts entwined,
Flames of love, pure and kind.

As we gather, voices blend,
In this circle, souls commend.
Unity in sacred space,
Flames of joy, we now embrace.

Spirit Set Aglow

In the silence, hear the call,
Spirit rising, we stand tall.
With every heartbeat, truth unspun,
In the darkness, we are one.

Echoes of love, soft and clear,
Drawn to grace, we banish fear.
From the ashes, life takes flight,
Spirit set aglow by light.

In the laughter, joy ignites,
Guiding us through starry nights.
With each prayer, we seek to find,
Heaven's touch in heart and mind.

Hands together, we will rise,
With each blessing, spirits prize.
In the warmth, the love bestowed,
Hearts united, all are whole.

Through the journey, we will soar,
Finding peace, forevermore.
As we walk, let faith increase,
Spirit set aglow in peace.

Flames of Hope Renewed

In the shadows, light will break,
Flames of hope, we shall awake.
Through the trials, we endure,
In God's promise, we are sure.

Every burden, cast away,
In His arms, we find our way.
With each heartbeat, dreams unfold,
In the warmth, the world is gold.

Raise your voice, let praises ring,
In sweet harmony, we sing.
As the dawn brings forth our song,
In His love, we all belong.

Beneath skies where blessings flow,
Flames of hope begin to glow.
In unity, our spirits shine,
Through the dark, our hearts align.

Dreamers gathered, hand in hand,
Winding pathways, love will stand.
In the light, our souls are steered,
Through the flames, hope is revered.

The Ember's Embrace

In the quiet glow of night,
The ember's warmth draws near,
A gentle whisper of His grace,
    Chasing away all fear.

Within the heart, a promise grows,
Through shadows it will gleam,
    The fire of love will ignite,
    Reviving every dream.

Each flicker tells a sacred tale,
Of hope and deep despair,
In every spark, His presence found,
    In stillness, fervent prayer.

Tonight we gather, hand in hand,
    United in the light,
We lift our voices to the skies,
With faith, we take to flight.

Through trials fierce, we'll find our way,
In embers, we are blessed,
With every heartbeat, we shall know,
In love, we'll find our rest.

Trials of the Soul

In valleys low, where shadows dwell,
Our spirits start to ache,
Yet in these times, we seek Him still,
Our burdens He will take.

With every challenge, strength emerges,
A blessing in disguise,
For in the heat of struggle's forge,
Our weary hearts shall rise.

His wisdom guides through paths unknown,
With faith, we find our way,
The trials faced, they shape our souls,
Transforming night to day.

So let us walk through fire and flame,
With courage, side by side,
For each step taken in His name,
Brings joy and holy pride.

In every tear, a lesson learned,
In every scar, a mark,
We journey on, through darkest hours,
To find the sacred spark.

Refined by Flames

In the furnace, I am called,
To face the heat of strife,
With every trial, I am changed,
The fire grants me life.

The flames reveal what lies within,
A heart of hidden gold,
As dross is burned away in time,
His promises unfold.

Through every loss, a gain is made,
In ashes, hope shall bloom,
For faith is forged in fervent heat,
And grace will banish gloom.

I rise from depths, renewed and free,
A vessel made for Him,
In flames of love, my spirit sings,
For I shall not grow dim.

In trials faced with shining grace,
I trust the path I tread,
For in this life, through fire I've learned,
That I am proudly led.

In the Crucible of Faith

In trials born, my faith will grow,
With every tear I cry,
In the crucible, I find the strength,
To rise and to defy.

Each moment's test, a chance to shine,
To trust in His design,
Through every storm that shakes my soul,
His love will be my sign.

The path is steep, the struggle real,
Yet courage fuels my quest,
For in His hands, I am remade,
A spirit truly blessed.

With steady heart, I embrace the fire,
The heat that shapes my way,
In surrender, peace is found,
To guide me day by day.

So let the trials come and go,
In faith, I find my grace,
For through the crucible, I rise,
To meet Him, face to face.

In the Heart of the Inferno

In the heart where flames do rage,
Souls are tested, torn from cage.
With a prayer, they seek the dawn,
Finding strength where hope is born.

Through the heat, a whisper calls,
Guiding hearts when darkness falls.
In the ashes, grace will gleam,
Resurrected from the dream.

Fires roar but do not consume,
Faith ignites, dispelling gloom.
Lift your spirit, let it soar,
In the heart, there's love and more.

Reaching out to grasp the light,
In the shadows, find your sight.
For the flame that burns within,
Leads you home, away from sin.

In surrender, find your song,
In the chaos, you belong.
Though the world may be unkind,
In the inferno, peace you'll find.

Echoes from the Sacred Forge

In the forge where spirits meld,
Hammers strike as truth is held.
From the fire, the metal bends,
Crafting tools for hearts to mend.

Echoes ring through sacred space,
Every note a mark of grace.
With each strike, the shadows wane,
In the light, we find no pain.

Forged with faith, our spirits sing,
In the heat, we find our wing.
Every trial, a song retold,
In the forge, we're shaped and bold.

With courage bound by holy might,
We stand ready for the fight.
In the echoes, hear the sound,
Of a love that knows no bound.

Let the sparks of joy ignite,
Bringing warmth to darkest night.
In the sacred forge we stand,
Crafted strong by God's own hand.

Spirit Burned, Spirit Born

In the ashes of desire,
We rise up, a soul on fire.
From the pain of lessons learned,
In the darkness, hope is burned.

Spirit burned, yet never lost,
In the flames, we pay the cost.
Through the heartache, light will break,
With each trial, new paths we make.

Born anew from flames so bright,
In the depths, we find our light.
From the wreckage, love takes flight,
Guiding us through endless night.

In surrender, we shall see,
All the ways we were set free.
For the fire shapes our will,
In the silence, love is still.

Spirit's journey, wild and wide,
In the blaze, we shall abide.
With each heartbeat, faith will form,
From the fire, we are reborn.

The Purging Light of Faith

In the depths of shadowed night,
Comes a beacon, pure and bright.
Though the world may seem unkind,
In the light, our peace we find.

Purging all that weighs us down,
In the light, we shed the crown.
Every burden, let it go,
In the faith, our hearts will grow.

Radiant hope within us glows,
As the river of mercy flows.
In its currents, find release,
In the light, prepare for peace.

Guided by a hand unseen,
In our hearts, the love is keen.
With each step in faith we take,
Find the joy in every ache.

Let the purging light refine,
In this journey, we align.
For through trials, we embrace,
In the faith, we find our grace.

Spirit's Resilience in the Burn

In trials of fire, the spirit does rise,
Strength ignited, a flame in the skies.
Through ashes we walk, reborn and anew,
With faith as our guide, each step we pursue.

When doubt seeks to quench the light of our heart,
We gather our courage, refuse to depart.
The heat may be fierce, yet love stands so tall,
In the depths of the burn, is the answer to call.

From embers and smoke, we find our way clear,
With purpose ignited, we cast out our fear.
With each fleeting moment, we learn and we grow,
In the furnace of faith, our resilience will show.

For life is a journey, a sacred embrace,
In struggles and strife, we uncover His grace.
When seasons are harsh, and shadows surround,
The spirit's resilience in love can be found.

So let us not waver when storms rage at sea,
With hearts intertwined, we shall live free.
In the burn we'll discover the power within,
A spirit unyielding, destined to win.

Fire's Embrace, Grace's Gift

In the heart of the fire, a vision unfolds,
A dance of the flames, a story retold.
With each flickering spark, the spirit ascends,
In the warmth of the blaze, true healing descends.

We stand in the light of this sacred embrace,
As pain turns to purpose, and fear meets grace.
In the chaos of heat, a whisper we hear,
A promise of hope that casts aside fear.

Through trials igniting the depths of our soul,
We gather the pieces, and out of control,
The fire transforms, with love's gentle kiss,
We're made whole again in this heavenly bliss.

With grace as our anchor, we rise from the ash,
The past now forgotten, no longer we clash.
In the fire's warm glow, we find our true path,
With hearts full of courage, we bloom from the wrath.

So let us be vessels, carrying light,
In the fire's embrace, we shall shine ever bright.
For in every struggle, a gift shall persist,
The fire's embrace, grace's loving twist.

Forged in the Divine Heat

In the furnace of faith, our hearts are refined,
Forged in the divine heat, our souls intertwined.
Every trial we face, is a step toward grace,
In the crucible of life, we find our true place.

With passion ignited, we rise from the flames,
Each challenge ignites, new love that proclaims.
In the trial's embrace, we are shaped and made whole,
A testament written, deep within our soul.

When storms of despair seek to darken our way,
In the heat we stand firm, no matter the fray.
With courage as armor, we march forth in love,
Forged in the fire, guided from above.

For every scar earned is a medal we wear,
A sign of resilience, a story to share.
In the presence of trials, we stand with pride,
In the divine heat, our spirits abide.

So let us be willing, to enter the flame,
With hearts open wide, we shall never feel shame.
For in the divine heat, our destiny's spun,
Every trial embraced, together we've won.

The Light of Shattered Chains

From darkness we rise, in chains we were bound,
But the light of His mercy can always be found.
With each shackle broken, our spirits take flight,
In the glow of His love, we emerge in the light.

With every confession, a chain shall be freed,
In the warmth of His grace, we find our true need.
For the weight of our burdens is lifted away,
As the light of shattered chains guides our way.

We dance through the shadows, our hearts full of song,
With love as our anthem, where we all belong.
In the light of forgiveness, we find our release,
In the face of His mercy, our souls find their peace.

No longer imprisoned by doubts or by fears,
In His tender embrace, we dry all our tears.
With every step forward, we claim our new name,
For the light of shattered chains ignites our flame.

So let us step boldly, with courage and grace,
In the light of His love, we'll forever find place.
For in every heart where His light has been sought,
The chains of our past are eternally caught.

The Sacred Flame

In the stillness of the night,
A flicker breaks the dark.
Its glow whispers a prayer,
Guiding hearts, igniting spark.

Beyond the shadows cast,
It dances with the light.
A beacon in the storm,
Leading souls to what's right.

In reverence, we gather,
Around this holy blaze.
A covenant of spirits,
In warmth, our spirits raise.

Through trials we will tread,
With faith our only guide.
The sacred flame within,
In love, we will abide.

So let it burn eternal,
A testimony of grace.
In every heart it dwells,
A light time can't erase.

Chosen by the Heat

Amidst the fiery trials,
The chosen ones arise.
They bear the weight of faith,
With steadfast hearts and eyes.

Through molten paths they walk,
Each step a sacred token.
Forged in the blazing fire,
The spirit never broken.

From ashes they will rise,
Each ember tells a tale.
Of courage born in flames,
In triumph, they prevail.

With wisdom gained from pain,
They shine a guiding light.
Chosen by the heat,
In darkness, they ignite.

Together they will stand,
In harmony and grace.
United by the fire,
In love, they find their place.

Baptism of Resilience

In water's cool embrace,
We shed the old, the past.
A baptism of the soul,
In faith, our hearts are cast.

The currents may be strong,
Yet deeper flows our trust.
We rise from waves of doubt,
In hope, we conquer rust.

Immerse us in the tides,
Let trials serve their way.
For through this test we grow,
In light, we choose to stay.

Emerging from the deep,
Each drop a blessing pure.
With spirits intertwined,
In love, we will endure.

So let the waters flow,
A sacred cleansing rite.
In unity, we find,
Strength born from our fight.

Ascending from the Hearth

From the hearth of our hearts,
The embers softly glow.
A warmth that fuels our dreams,
In faith, we rise and grow.

With every breath we take,
We fan the flames anew.
United with a purpose,
In courage, we'll break through.

As smoke rises to the sky,
Our spirits take to flight.
We soar on wings of love,
In trust, we seek the light.

Through seasons of our lives,
The hearth will always be.
A place of hope and grace,
Where hearts forever free.

So let us gather 'round,
In reverence, hand in hand.
Ascending from the hearth,
In unity we stand.

Milton Keynes UK
Ingram Content Group UK Ltd.
UKHW020039271124
451585UK00012B/948